BAD LIES

BAD LIES

A FIELD GUIDE TO
LOST BALLS, MISSING LINKS,
AND OTHER GOLF MISHAPS

CHARLES LINDSAY

Foreword by Gary McCord
"Anima Orbis" by Timothy Tate

LITTLE, BROWN AND COMPANY

NEW YORK   BOSTON   LONDON

THIS BOOK IS DEDICATED TO BAD LIES AND THE MEN AND WOMEN WHO COMMIT THEM.

AND TO ALL THE FRIENDS I'VE MADE THROUGH THIS GAME: YOU HAVE GIVEN ME SUCH PLEASURE WHILE I HAVE ENDURED SUCH PAIN.

Also by Charles Lindsay
Lost Balls: Great Holes, Tough Shots, and Bad Lies
Upstream: Fly-Fishing in the American West
Turtle Islands: Balinese Ritual and the Green Turtle
Mentawai Shaman: Keeper of the Rain Forest

Little, Brown and Company
Hachette Book Group
237 Park Avenue, New York, NY 10017
www.hachettebookgroup.com

First Edition: May 2010

Little, Brown and Company is a division of Hachette Book Group, Inc. The Little, Brown name and logo are trademarks of Hachette Book Group, Inc.

Library of Congress Cataloging-in-Publication Data
Lindsay, Charles.
  Bad lies : a field guide to lost balls, missing links, and other golf mishaps / Charles Lindsay, Gary McCord.
    p. cm.
ISBN 978-0-316-07419-3
1. Golf — Pictorial works. 2. Golf — Anecdotes. 3. McCord, Gary. I. Title.
GV967.5.L54 2010
796.352 — dc22   2009028709

10 9 8 7 6 5 4 3 2 1

Printed in Singapore

PAGE 2: 17TH HOLE, THE CLUB AT BLACK ROCK, COEUR D'ALENE, IDAHO

Lie

The condition of the ball when it is not in motion during a game of golf. Good lies include a level stretch of pristine fairway or anywhere the ball sits up and the player has an unobstructed swing. Balls plugged in sand traps, sunk in water hazards, perched on thorn bushes, and knee-deep in the rough are examples of bad lies.

Gary McCord

In my thirty-five years of playing professional golf, with a modicum of decorum, I have withstood humiliation and angst beyond the imaginable. I have prepared myself mentally, physically, emotionally, and spiritually for the game, and yet still I can't cope with the serendipitous whims of my golf ball. Things go off course (so to speak), and I tend to start whining hysterically.

I remember with chagrin and not a small amount of discomfort several occasions when my golf ball became engaged in extracurricular activities on the PGA Tour. These occasions were too numerous to be chalked up to coincidence.

Once I entered a greenside bunker at the Milwaukee Open with a palpable confidence. I was only three shots out of the lead and needed to get it close, but I was certain I had what it would take. After sizing up the situation and getting a feel for my thirty-foot blast, I let go with a precise strike and turned my sand wedge into a 7 iron. The ball flew over the green, over the terrified gallery, both of them, and zoomed over a village of port-a-johns with amazing velocity. I manfully walked in the general direction of the golf ball's path and came upon a hot dog stand that had a certain buzz about it. They directed me to the front of the line where a gentleman had mustard and relish spread over his face like a bad rash. "Looking for your ball?" He pointed toward the condiment tray; there it lay in all its disruptive glory. A bad lie.

17TH TEE BOX, GOLF HOUSE CLUB, ELIE, SCOTLAND

Another time I was playing a golf tournament at Pebble Beach called "The Crosby," after its founder, Bing Crosby. We were on the 16th hole at Cypress Point Golf Club, the most spectacular par three in the world. That day it was playing 217 yards across the Pacific Ocean with the wind whispering in my left ear at around 17 knots. I was dazed and confused, but without hesitation I aroused some clubhead speed with my 3 iron and majestically put the ball in the sand . . . on a beach seventy yards to the left of the green. The sound of my golf ball embedding itself in the seashells and sand woke up a slumbering seal a few feet away. He gracefully waddled aside, allowing me to play through.

How I got there I don't quite know, but I eventually found myself standing next to my ball on the beach, getting directions to the general vicinity of the flag from my caddy. He was standing sentinel on the ledge in front of me when a rogue wave hit me from behind and unceremoniously deposited me and my golf ball back into the Pacific Ocean. The sea lions on a nearby rock outcropping barked with enthusiasm. They love bad lies.

Curiously, I find that leafing through the pages of Charles Lindsay's pictorial playbook on unacceptable lies and long-forgotten golf balls has given me some solace. I now can accept the fact that other people have had the ball roll into a jousting, jumping cholla cactus or land in a colorful bush a mere thirty-seven yards off the fairway, with a mockingbird sitting in a nearby tree, cackling at your efforts to extricate the orb from said bush. Strength is in numbers.

A bad lie is just that. It's a test of our resolve. It is something we all have to deal with from time to time, unless you're like a buddy of mine named "Winter Rules" Walter. His golf ball always ended up perched. This book is not for Walt. This book is for the rest of us. Those who have suffered the indignity of a perfectly manicured fairway with a clean coat of new winter rye on a crisp spring day and a drive hit somewhere near the center of the club that reaches the bottom of a divot. We can look at these pictures and derive a certain amount of satisfaction from knowing that one man's bad lie is another man's pay dirt.

Charles Lindsay has embarked on a quixotic journey to document the ups and downs and ins and outs of a seemingly innocuous white ball (and a few orange and pink ones, some emblazoned with very odd messages) and its constant conflict with the prepared environment in which it ricochets. At least that's what mine does. I salute you, Mr. Lindsay, for capturing, in vivid color, those demons that sent me to the broadcast booth. I salute you, with one finger exposed.

JUMPING CHOLLA CACTUS AT TROON GOLF CLUB, SCOTTSDALE, ARIZONA

BAD LIES

Double Bogey

Don't play it again, Sam. Two strokes over par.
A double-bogey golfer would score 36 over par
on an eighteen-hole round—just breaking 100.
God help him.

AL'S SOCKS, EL BORRACHO TOURNAMENT AT SANCTUARY GOLF COURSE, SEDALIA, COLORADO

DICK ESTEY (IN CART) AND FRIEND (OVER A LIMB) AT WAVERLEY COUNTRY CLUB, PORTLAND, OREGON
OPPOSITE: LUNDIN GOLF CLUB, LUNDIN LINKS, SCOTLAND

Birdie

One stroke below par. A common refrain of the
senile player: "Here birdie, birdie . . ."

STARTER LOOKING TO SEE IF THE BLIND LANDING ZONE AT THE 1ST HOLE IS CLEAR, USING SALVAGED SUBMARINE PERISCOPE, ELIE GOLF HOUSE CLUB, ELIE, SCOTLAND

BUNKER IN THE 12TH GREEN AT DOONBEG, A GREG NORMAN–DESIGNED LINKS COURSE, DOONBEG, IRELAND

Come-backer

The putt you take after you have hit the ball
past the hole. Miss this one and you are toast.

Water Hazard

Any substantial body of water within the boundaries of the course—whether lake, pond, sea, fountain, or drainage ditch. A system of devious conspiracies between golf-course architects, church ministers, and CEOs intended solely to aid the golf-ball manufacturing business and church donations through the torment of golfers.

DUNKED DRIVE, FOREST HIGHLANDS GOLF CLUB, FLAGSTAFF, ARIZONA

PLEASE RING BELL

1ST TEE, FISHERMEN'S COURSE, BARRA GOLF CLUB, ISLE OF BARRA, SCOTLAND
OPPOSITE: WARNING BELL, ENNISCRONE GOLF CLUB, ENNISCRONE, IRELAND

Featherie

An antique, hand-sewn leather golf ball that was, in fact, filled with a "hatful" of goose feathers. The featherie was popular up until the late 1840s, when it was phased out with the introduction of the gutta percha ball. Today, an authentic featherie ball can fetch hundreds of thousands of dollars at auction.

NINETEENTH-CENTURY FEATHERIE BALL

BEWARE. of Golfers
BEREHAVEN GOLF CLUB

BEREHAVEN GOLF CLUB ENTRY, COUNTY CORK, IRELAND
OPPOSITE: DAVID AND SECURITY CAMERA, 7TH HOLE, BIGHORN GOLF CLUB, MOUNTAINS COURSE, PALM DESERT, CALIFORNIA

Downhill Lie

The ball (or, in some instances, the golfer) has come to rest on a downhill slope in the direction of play.

SEARCHING THE SEA WALL, NORTH BERWICK GOLF CLUB, EAST LOTHIAN, SCOTLAND

GREENSIDE BUNKER BLAST, 8TH HOLE, THE TUXEDO CLUB, TUXEDO PARK, NEW YORK

Murphy's Law

What can go wrong will go wrong.

Gorse

Thick, tangled, and aggressively spiked evergreen shrub found at many ocean-side links. Gorse is believed to have made its way from Ireland to the West Coast of the United States on early schooners. It blossoms bright yellow in the spring and has thorns to dissuade anyone from becoming friendly with it.

HEAVY GORSE, BANDON DUNES GOLF RESORT, BANDON, OREGON
FOLLOWING PAGES: 18TH HOLE, OLD TABBY LINKS, SPRING ISLAND, SOUTH CAROLINA

ALLIGATOR AND ERRANT BALL, OLD TABBY LINKS, SPRING ISLAND, SOUTH CAROLINA

Away

The golfer whose ball is positioned farthest from the hole is said to be "away." The Rules of Golf dictate that the player who is away plays first. Also called "out." The term may also be used of a player at the nineteenth hole who has had a few too many drinks.

SALTON SEA PUBLIC GOLF COURSE, SALTON CITY, CALIFORNIA

THUNDERBIRD COUNTRY CLUB, PHOENIX, ARIZONA

Gutta Percha

A rubbery substance made from the resin of the tropical Sapodilla tree that was used to form the core material of golf balls from the late 1840s until the early 1900s. A gutta percha ball is often referred to as a "gutty."

Fried Egg

Slang for a ball half-buried in the sand. Popping the
ball out of a fried egg requires one of golf's most
challenging shots—a precise opening of the club face
and a swing that digs in at an angle.

BALL CAUGHT IN AN UNREPAIRED FOOTPRINT, RYDER COURSE, PGA VILLAGE, PORT ST. LUCIE, FLORIDA

PROFESSIONAL GOLF BALL COLLECTOR, THE TUXEDO CLUB, TUXEDO PARK, NEW YORK

OVERLEAF: LEFT PAGE, TOP ROW: HENLEY MESH PATTERN, 1890s. HENRY'S RIFLED, 1902, FROM THE HARRY B. WOOD COLLECTION; EXTREMELY VALUABLE. FAROID, THIS END UP, 1930s; DESIGNED TO REDUCE SLICES AND HOOKS. MIDDLE ROW: BLUE WINTER BALL, 1890s. ARMY & NAVY, EARLY 1900s. HASKELL, 1899, FROM THE HARRY B. WOOD COLLECTION; THE FIRST RUBBER-CORED BALL TO BE MASS-PRODUCED. BOTTOM ROW: THE DUPLEX. T-DIMPLE GUTTY. SPIRAL PATTERN.

OVERLEAF: RIGHT PAGE, TOP ROW: THE LUNAR. BOXWOOD BALL, 15TH CENTURY (?). COARSE HATCH PATTERN, EARLY 1900s. MIDDLE ROW: SPIRAL PAINTED GUTTY, EARLY 1900s. RED WINTER BALL, HAND-HAMMERED GUTTY, 1855. SILVER KING S BRAMBLE, 1890s. BOTTOM ROW: BLUE CROSS PRACTICE BALL. WILLIE DUNN'S STARS AND STRIPES, 1897. U.S. TIGER BALL, 1930.

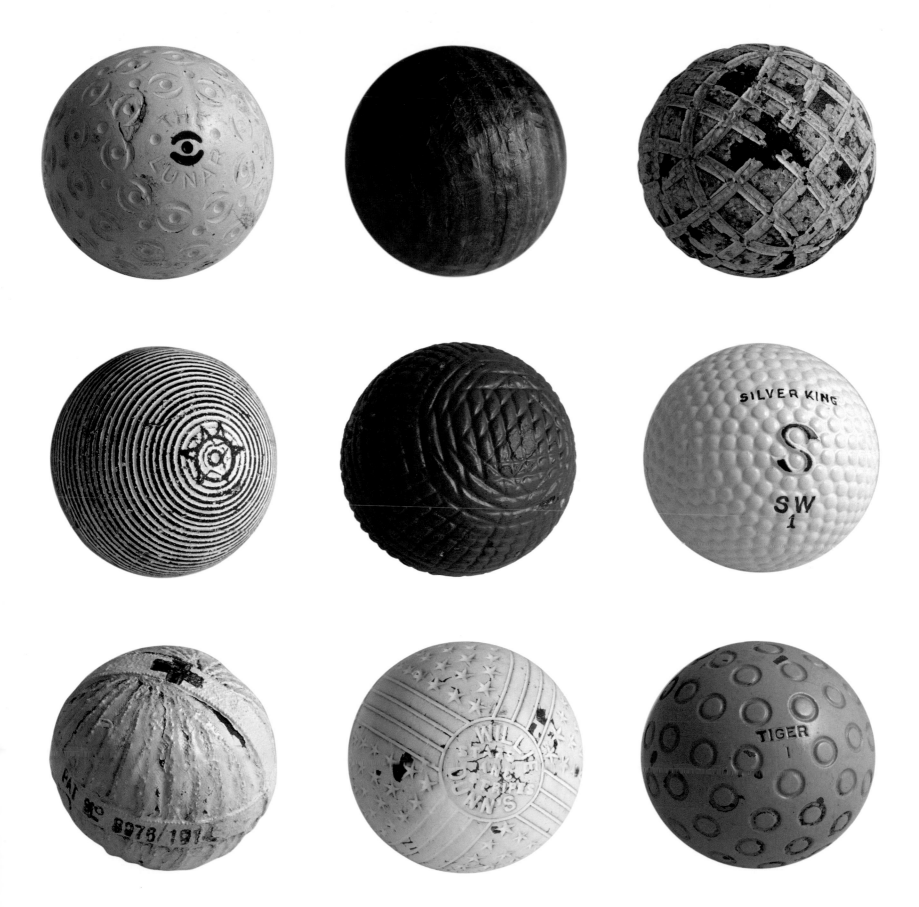

TERRESTRIAL GLOBE OR "MAP OF THE WORLD" BRAMBLE BALLS. UNPAINTED (LEFT) AND PAINTED, 1908

TOP LEFT: RED LEATHER FEATHERIE, A WINTER BALL, LATE 1840s. TOP RIGHT: ZOME TWO, EARLY 20TH CENTURY.
BOTTOM LEFT: JAPANESE GLASS BALL, 1950s. BOTTOM RIGHT: SNAKESKIN BALL OR "TEXAS FEATHERIE," 1990s.

Hosel

On a golf club, the region where the club head connects to the shaft. Hitting the ball off the hosel is called a shank or, alternately, a hosel rocket.

Unplayable Lie

A ball that has landed in a location or hazard that renders it impossible to play has achieved an unplayable lie. In most instances the player may choose to replay the ball from his last position or to drop the ball to within two club lengths of where it has landed, not nearer the hole. In either case, a penalty of one stroke is applied.

BALL DISCOVERED IN A TREE CROTCH, RYDER COURSE, PGA VILLAGE, PORT ST. LUCIE, FLORIDA

GOLF CARTS AT BIGHORN GOLF CLUB, PALM DESERT, CALIFORNIA

STACK'S MOTEL AND DRIVING RANGE, EAST DURHAM, NEW YORK

Bramble

A type of golf ball manufactured in Great Britain in the mid-nineteenth century, said to be named after the fruit found on brambles in the English countryside. The bramble was made of gutta percha (a tropical tree sap) and covered with an irregular bramble pattern that aided the ball's flight. The bramble is the forerunner of the modern dimpled golf ball.

TOM MORRIS PAINTED BRAMBLE BALL, CIRCA 1906

Fore!

What you should shout immediately after your swing if you think an errant shot may hit a player or a spectator. You must yell loudly and in time for your warning to be effective.

MICHELLE WIE ON THE PRACTICE RANGE WITH HER DAD, AFTER THE KRAFT NABISCO CHAMPIONSHIP
OPPOSITE: WELCOME SIGN, SALTON SEA PUBLIC GOLF COURSE, SALTON CITY, CALIFORNIA

SMILEY FACE BALL, TIMELESS
OPPOSITE: NATALIE GULBIS ON THE 9TH GREEN, KRAFT NABISCO CHAMPIONSHIP, MISSION HILLS COUNTRY CLUB, RANCHO MIRAGE, CALIFORNIA

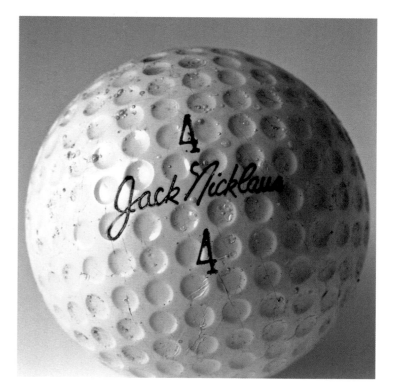

THIS SPREAD: 1940–70s PRO ENDORSEMENTS AND A PREMONITION—THE TIGER BALL PRE-DATES HIS ARRIVAL IN PRO GOLF

Ball

A sphere ranging from 1.62 to 1.68 inches in diameter made of compressed rubber and covered with indentations (called dimples) that is the center of attention in the game of golf. Modern golf balls are traditionally white, but many other colors are also used. Brand names, logos, and custom imprinting help players personalize their balls and distinguish one from another. Many golfers believe that golf balls have been invented specifically to be lost.

Dance Floor

An informal term for the putting green. After a long shot from the fairway, you hope to hear that you are on the dance floor. Even then you are likely dancing with a guy who wears ridiculous clothing and has knobby knees.

ANIMA ORBIS
Or, How an Ordinary Golf Ball and
a Golfer's Immortal Soul Are One and the Same

Timothy Tate

Easy now, slow the thoughts down, look at the back of the ball, steady, big guy. Trust the body's wisdom, it knows what to do. Be quiet and swing low, sweet driver. The wee white orb sits nonchalantly atop its tee—silent, detached, unmoved, patiently waiting: "Strike me if you dare. Give me your best shot. I'm all yours."

Such thoughts, heard only by the golfer, race around the brain. A silent, wrenching, personal dialog. Facing the gleaming ball on the first tee box brings this unspoken inner conversation to the boiling mind's forefront. Hold on, was that a thought or was it screamed out loud? It sounded so intense. The three men watching from two club lengths away didn't seem to notice. But is there snickering?

The unspoken chatter brewing in this white-ball, green-turf moment matures over a lifetime into soulfulness or disintegrates into babbling madness: "460cc driver my ass; it looks like a goddamn well-shined titanium clubfoot." The soul needs a workout in order to mature, and golf is its perfect match: "Stay calm? Hell, I'm one move away from murder." If the Greeks were right and the persona must be taken apart for us to comprehend its true character, then this 220-yard, par-three waterhole is its operating theater. A little dimpled ball holds fate in its lie. How can something so small hold so much gravity?

I have considered a possible answer: that the weight of the golf ball and the weight of the soul are one and the same, 21 grams. The concept dates back to the early twentieth century, when a certain Dr. MacDougall weighed dying patients precisely at the moment of death, as the soul was purported to be leaving the body. The differential, in body mass before and after, averaged 21 grams, which is the exact minimum official weight of a golf ball.

From the Scots on the links swinging hand-hewn persimmon mashies at a "gentleman's hat full of feathers," to hard-hitting professionals on the PGA tour using composite drivers to launch the weightiest modern Pro Vs, the soul and sphere have traveled in tandem.

Of course, the soul of modern man is heavier than it used to be in those lost Brigadoon mists of St. Andrews fairways. So the Rules of Golf have evolved to accommodate up to 45 grams. Nonetheless, the age-old challenge still haunts us.

The perfect golf shot, like a Zen koan, makes silent contact with the ball, sending it soaring to exactly where the mind's eye saw it going. Such moments of grace arise from the union of a golfer's apparent effortlessness and the orb's "unbearable lightness of being." Whose swing will lift that soul-orb toward the cup today?

A VERY RARE INTACT FEATHERIE, SIGNED "ST. ANDREWS OCTOBER 1839"

Sand Trap

Unofficial term for a bunker, specifically a bunker in the vicinity of the green that is filled with sand, as opposed to a grass bunker. Also referred to as "the beach."

Fescue

A tall, tufted grass, golden in color, that is often grown in the rough alongside fairways in the U.S. and U.K. Fescue pollen is a major contributor to hay fever. Hitting golf balls into fescue is a major source of nervous disorders in golfers.

HUSBAND AND WIFE IN LONG ROUGH, BACK NINE, ENNISCRONE GOLF CLUB, ENNISCRONE, IRELAND

A BADLY BEATEN BRAMBLE BALL, CIRCA 1890s

IN THE BANYAN TREES, 14TH HOLE, SEMINOLE GOLF CLUB, JUNO BEACH, FLORIDA

Out of Bounds

The area outside the boundaries of the golf course, usually indicated by fencing or white stakes. Players are penalized one stroke if their ball is entirely out of bounds, and they must take another shot from the original shot's location—hence "three off the tee" is what you hit after your drive goes OB.

BLACKTAIL DEER AT SPYGLASS HILL GOLF COURSE, PEBBLE BEACH, CALIFORNIA
OPPOSITE: GOLF BALL HUNTER GIVES BACK, 5TH HOLE, THE TUXEDO CLUB, TUXEDO PARK, NEW YORK

Links

Technically, a golf course along the ocean, built on nonarable land. Links are notorious for their high winds and tricky terrain. These courses tend not to require the level of pesticide and fertilizer use that "parklands" courses require. More brown, less green, more natural. However, "links" has also come into common usage as a generic term for golf course. The missing link is another story.

ONE OF HUNDREDS OF LOST GOLF BALLS ON THE BEACH BELOW THE CLIFFS AT BANDON AND PACIFIC DUNES GOLF COURSES, BANDON, OREGON
PRECEDING PAGES: LOOKING FOR LOST DRIVES ON THE "LONG BANK," 16TH HOLE AT ENNISCRONE GOLF CLUB, ENNISCRONE, IRELAND

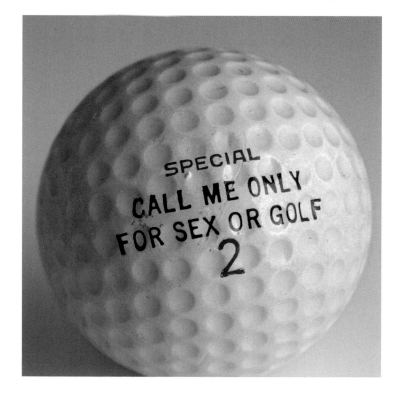

AS IF THE GAME WEREN'T ENOUGH TO HUMBLE US, HERE ARE SOME REMINDERS

LUNAR LANDING COMMEMORATIVE BALL, CIRCA 1970

Hole

A circular opening on the putting green from which a flagstick extends and into which the player hopes to hit the ball. Also called "the cup," it is 4.25 inches in diameter. To "go in the hole" is the ultimate achievement in golf, until it doesn't.

Chili Dipping

Slang term for hitting a "fat" shot in which the club face strikes the ground, usually catching more ground than ball. Also called a "chunk." The result of a lowered shoulder, chili dipping is unpleasant to witness and physically draining to the dipper when repeated.

CHRIS TAKES A DIVOT AT OLD TABBY LINKS, SPRING ISLAND, SOUTH CAROLINA

FOX-CHEWED STRATA BALL, CARNE, IRELAND

OTTER AND LOST BALLS AT OLD MARSH GOLF CLUB, PALM BEACH GARDENS, FLORIDA

Dunch

No, not a meal sneaked in between lunch and dinner but, in archaic British golf parlance, a fat hit from a claggy lie. What's "claggy," you ask? That would be muddy, or sticky, of course.

THE 6TH TEE AND BALL HOLDER AT CONNEMARA CHAMPIONSHIP GOLF LINKS, COUNTY GALWAY, IRELAND
OPPOSITE: MUSHROOMS AT PGA VILLAGE, PORT ST. LUCIE, FLORIDA

Mulligan

A minor slipup with a no-penalty repeat that is permitted through the goodwill of opponents or pals. It usually occurs on the first tee, where it is presumed that one is not warmed up or where the evil and as-yet-unexorcised yips are most likely to surface.

THE CHALLENGER BALL MADE BY COCHRANE, EARLY 1900s
OPPOSITE: BALLS IN TUMBLEWEED ON THE CLIFFS AT BLUE LAKES GOLF COURSE, TWIN FALLS, IDAHO

Bird's Nest

Said of a golf ball nestled in tall grass. The opposite
of a bare lie. In rare cases golf balls have ended up
in actual bird's nests.

13TH GREEN, BIGHORN GOLF CLUB AND COMMUNITY, PALM DESERT, CALIFORNIA

WELCOME SIGN, THE CLUBHOUSE AT SALTON SEA PUBLIC COURSE, SALTON CITY, CALIFORNIA

Worm Burner

A ball hit hard and low, staying airborne just a few feet off the ground and traveling an impressive distance. It may skip, much like a flat rock across a calm lake surface. Beware this shin-high shot.

TEE BOX AT BIGHORN GOLF CLUB, MOUNTAIN COURSE, PALM DESERT, CALIFORNIA

TEE BOX AT 9-HOLE SALTON SEA PUBLIC COURSE, SALTON CITY, CALIFORNIA

Zinger

A ball hit especially hard and low. Useful when
hitting into the wind.

Nineteenth Hole

At the end of a round of golf (eighteen holes), this is the clubhouse bar. The setting for many an excuse, exaggeration, lie.

AFTERWORD
Charles Lindsay

After a satisfying round of golf you walk into an ancient pub and resolutely crack your head on the low doorframe. The hobbits that invented the game are still initiating you. If this isn't more fun than being driven around the countryside in the backseat of a first-generation Mini with a set of antique clubs poking your ribs, what is? But perhaps the trolls have that in store for you later on. Better drink the stout. Here we go again.

You could call it bad luck, but in fact a bad lie can only be pilot error, because those of us who golf have chosen a game in which the equipment is too basic to blame. Here lies a perfect metaphor for the classic heroic struggle. The game of golf is Good versus Evil, plain and simple. Redemption will require imagination, talent, some measure of restraint, humor, and, of course, some good luck.

We all know a round of golf is seldom *all* good luck, but I have played with Seniors who seem to circumvent Murphy's Law. They exhibit something equivalent to wisdom, the existence of which has been proven by scientists—and not the same ones who engineer golf balls to go to the moon! These Seniors don't swing hard and don't hit the ball far, but it goes down the middle over and over again and they score low, leaving the herculean duffer in their wakes . . . over in the bushes with the snakes.

In the name of golf I've endangered my friends, brought them to tears, singed their ears, spoken in tongues, offered unsolicited advice (and then not heeded it myself), stepped in the poop, looked up, swung too hard, aligned overly left (easy for me), and aligned overly right (not so easy but far more hazardous). Time and again . . . why this bloody game?

So once again I decided to give my clubs a rest and picked up my cameras instead—to really pay attention to the acts and artifacts of golf. To my surprise it suddenly seemed that everything and everybody was looking at the game. At many tournaments there are TV cameras, still cameras, mobile videophones, binoculars, periscopes, security cameras, blimps, spy satellites, mirrored sunglasses, and, on occasion, those out-of-fashion naked eyeballs. There are golf-specific talking heads, reality-show dudes, self-help infomercials, and then afterward those annoying junk e-mails trying to sell us gizmos and gadgets galore—all

promising the final secret. A chip embedded in a high-tech golf ball now allows its owner to locate it via GPS.

What happened to raising a saliva-wetted finger to determine the direction of the wind's knots before shaping a shot? Relax, they say. How is that possible? Even the animal kingdom is paying attention: otters, deer, turkeys, alligators, chipmunks, and hawks up high, all observing our moves, mocking our foibles and groans.

Through this project I came into contact with serious golf ball collectors—yes, they do exist—the keepers and traders of the remaining relics that have not been locked up in museums. Some of the balls I photographed are worth tens, even hundreds, of thousands of dollars. It boggles the mind. When we see an object or a picture of an object, something actually touched by Old Tom Morris, what meaning does it transmit?

A ball, a skipping stone, a Frisbee, a boomerang—all physical embodiments of memories, these remnants of actual deeds and of evolution in sport. The rarer the object the more valuable, we take that for granted, but stop for a moment to think about

it. The perception of value that casts its golden glow on these objects exists only within that three-inch-wide golf course between our ears—the one that Lee Trevino designed, or was it God? I forget who, actually. How far can we hit the ball, how far can we propel our minds . . . into the past, into the future?

I have tried to make photographs that suggest a shared experience, where the viewer connects to a common occurrence on the fairway or green, a universal mishap and ultimately, hopefully, a smile afterward. If I've succeeded, the image is no longer mine; you enter the picture and make it your own. Recent neuro-logical experiments have shown that our memories are rebuilt every time we access them. And that is a beautiful image, because memory, not unlike a photo-graph, becomes the truth we tell ourselves.

INDIVIDUAL GUTTA PERCHA BALL MOULD, LATE 1800s

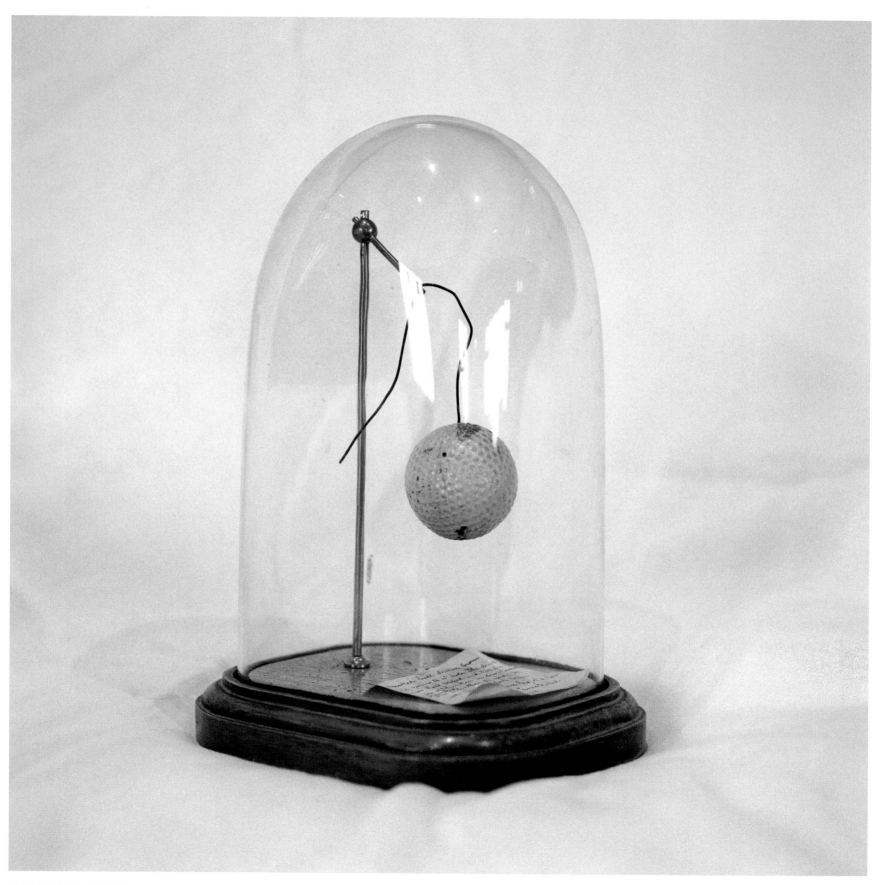

BRAMBLE BALL PRESERVED FROM AN INCIDENT IN THE 1890s IN WHICH A GOLFER'S ERRANT SHOT ALLEGEDLY HIT A PASSERBY ON THE HEAD AND IMPALED ITSELF UPON HER HAIRPIN. IN THE COLLECTION OF THE NORTH BERWICK GOLF CLUB, SCOTLAND.

ACKNOWLEDGMENTS

Many people who helped me with *Lost Balls* influenced this, its sequel. Michael Sand took my concept and shaped it with imagination, wit, and intelligence. There's nobody better in the business. THANK YOU, Michael.

Thanks to Miko McGinty for the handsome book design, and to the talented crew at Little, Brown and Company for publishing me so well.

Carrie Boretz and Jesse Reiter at *Golf Magazine* helped me with an introduction to Donna Hahn at the Kraft Nabisco Tournament and an assignment to photograph there. What a pleasure. Thank you all. David and Leisa Austin at Imago Galleries in Palm Desert were the most gracious hosts imaginable. David, sorry about pelting the houses at Bighorn. Good thing the Director of Member Relations there, Alan Skuba, is such a nice guy! Larry Bohannan sent me off to the Salton Sea after I made a comment about loving primitive golf—thanks, Larry! Hal and Wendy Greene, thank you for your constant smiles and kindness.

Thanks to those who appear in my photos and/or made suggestions that led to photographs: Patricia Savin at North Berwick; Martin Walsh in Connemara; Ken Murray, the starter at Elie; James Colo at Old Marsh; Drew Annan at Forest Highlands; Mark Clark at Troon Golf and Country Club; Dave Liniger and Rudy Zupetz at The Sanctuary; Joellen Zeh at Audubon International; Jim and Betsy Chaffin at Spring Island and Old Tabby Links; and Bill Sampson, Glenys Ryan, and Seth Zeigler. Thanks to Joel Waller and Tim Obenchain at Blue Lakes Country Club, to Rick Martino, golf teacher extraordinaire, to Bob Ford at Seminole Golf Club, Chris Lane and Terry Cook at Spyglass, Ken Nice at Bandon Dunes, and Ron Olsen and Trevor Fox at The Club at Black Rock. And I can't forget Dr. Al King—the sock images don't do you justice. Thanks again to Tim Foote, Timothy Tate, and Dick Purinton.

I owe a very special thanks to the group of collectors and historians who welcomed me into their circle to photograph and learn about their passion. This began with Rick Hartbrought, who introduced me to Joe Tiscornia, who sadly passed away too young—but not before introducing me to Dr. David Malcolm and Dick Estey and his wife, Judy, who in turn led me to Jim Espinola. Thank you all for your trust and smiles.

My great friend Jim Engh is an incredible golf course architect. Who would imagine that a guy who hits the ball so far could have such artistic sensibilities? Jim designs hazards so gorgeous you want to be in them. It was also Jim who introduced me to Gary McCord. Enormous thanks to both of you.

To the guys and gals I golf with annually in Sun Valley, Idaho—Jeff, Howard, Jeff, Hal, Victor, Gail, Benedict, Jeri, Mary, Steve, Geoff, Mike—thanks for putting up with me. To Greg Seitz at Elkhorn Golf Club, belated happy fortieth birthday! Dave Faltings and Terry Ring—let's go fishing instead.

Heartfelt thanks go to my wife, Catherine Chalmers, the smartest and most beautiful influence on me ever, and to our great friend Geoff Isles. Both have endured much via my golf-related exploits. Thanks to Frank Contey and David Carazo at The Tuxedo Club, and to Susan Winter for her stylish look on the green. The professional golf ball collector emerging from the pond at Tuxedo is Jeff Chatfield. Snapping turtles beware!

I am grateful to have golfed and shared laughs with John Updike, whose essay graced the pages of *Lost Balls*. I hope the greens run true and not too fast wherever you are.

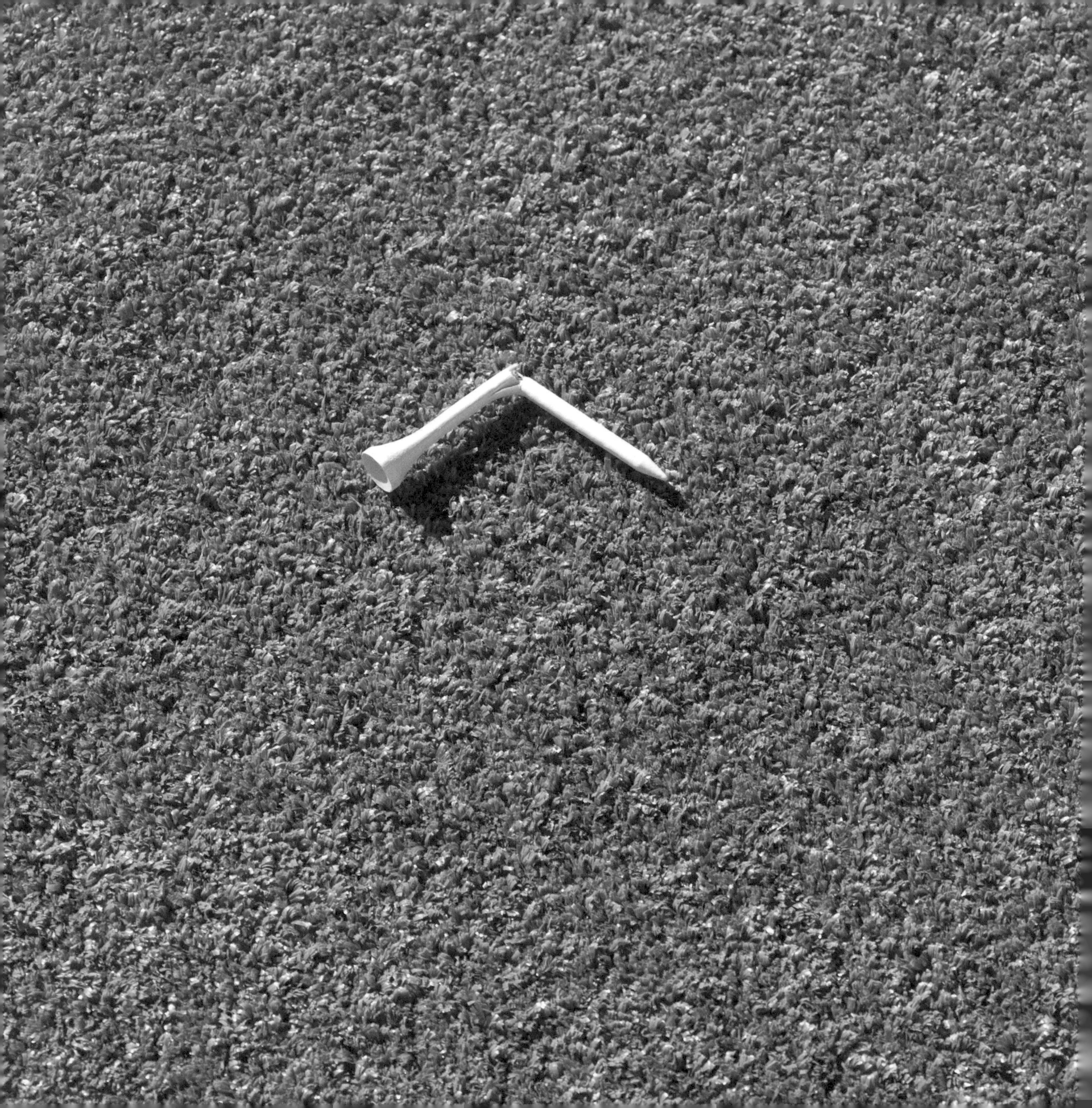